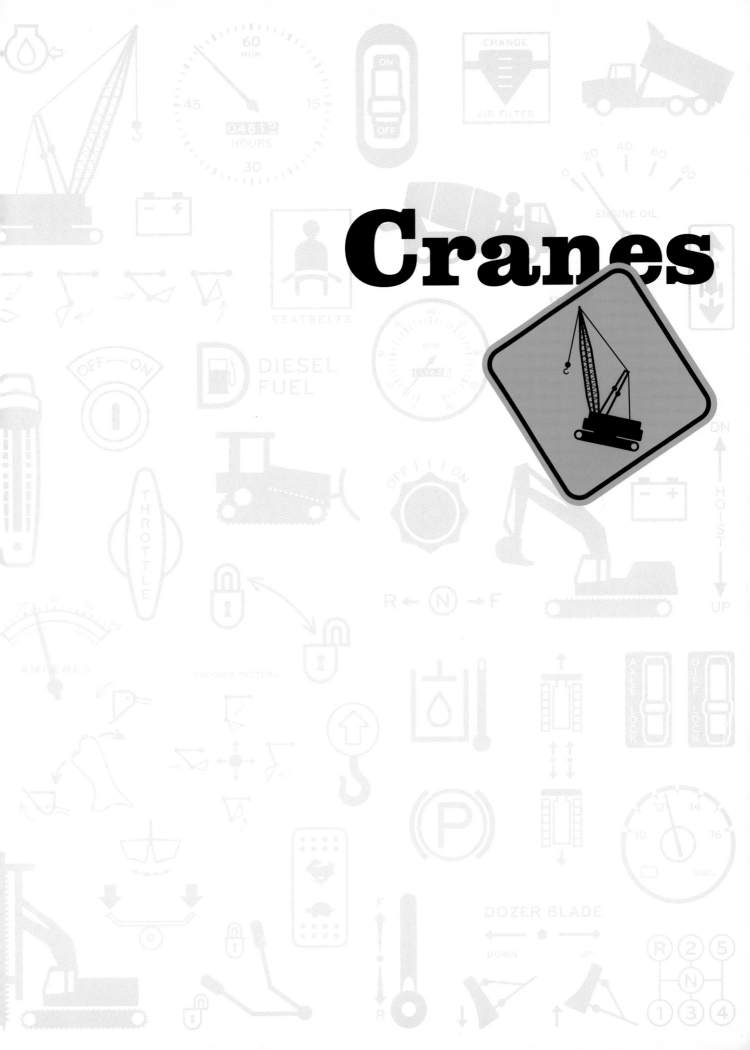

Cranes

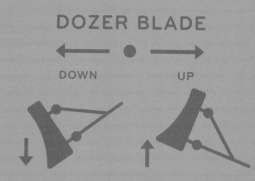

DOZER BLADE

DOWN   UP

Published by Creative Education
P.O. Box 227, Mankato, Minnesota 56002
Creative Education is an imprint of The Creative Company
www.thecreativecompany.us

Design and production by Rob & Damia Design
Art direction by Rita Marshall
Printed in the United States of America

Photographs by iStockphoto (Terry J. Alcorn, Mike Clarke, Patrick Fagan,
Majoros Laszlo, Paulo Resende, Peter Seager, John Sfondilias, Robert Simon,
Sergei Sverdelov, Teun Van den Dries), Damia Stewart/Rob & Damia Design

Library of Congress Cataloging-in-Publication Data

Gilbert, Sara.
Cranes / by Sara Gilbert.
p. cm. — (Machines that build)
Includes index.
ISBN 978-1-58341-727-0
1. Cranes, derricks, etc.—Juvenile literature. I. Title. II. Series.

TJ1363.G535 2009
621.8'73—dc22   2007051661

First edition
9 8 7 6 5 4 3 2 1

DIESEL
FUEL

OFF / / / / ON

ENGINE OIL

SEATBELTS

CREATIVE  EDUCATION

Cranes

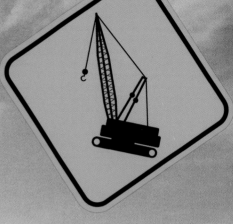

sara gilbert
machines that build

Cranes are tall machines with long, metal arms. They rise above construction (*con-STRUK-shun*) sites. Builders use cranes for lots of jobs.

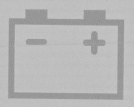

The arm of a crane is made out of strong metal.

Cranes can lift heavy things
that nothing else can.

Cranes can carry metal beams, chunks of concrete, and even boats! They load things onto ships and trains and *salvage* sunken ships. Cranes can help build new buildings. They can help tear down old ones, too.

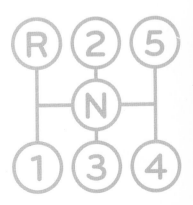

THROTTLE

Crane towers stand up tall. A long arm reaches out from the tower.

Tools hang from a strong **cable** on the arm.

Buckets and hooks are tools that cranes use.

Cranes use wrecking balls and magnets, too.

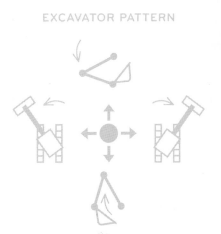

EXCAVATOR PATTERN

A crane operator

Crane **operators** sit in a *cab*. Sometimes the cab is high above the ground. The operator has to climb a long ladder to reach it. The operator controls the arm and the tools that hang on the arm.

Heavy hooks hang from chains on this crane's arm.

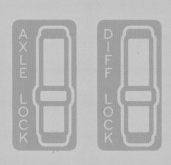

Some cranes rise almost 300 feet (91 m) into the air. Their arms can be more than 200 feet (61 m) long. Cranes have legs to hold them steady while they work.

Sometimes cranes look like tall balance beams.

13

Cranes have been around for a long time. In the *Middle Ages*, people made cranes to help them load ships. Early cranes were made of wood. People and animals had to use their muscles to move the cranes.

Cranes can reach over the tops of tall buildings.

*Many cranes are placed
close to where boats dock.*

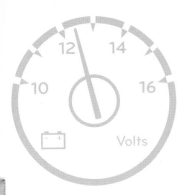

Today, cranes are powered by engines and motors. They can be carried by trucks or trains. Cranes can even float in the water. Helicopters carry some cranes into hard-to-reach places. The helicopters hold on to the cranes while they work.

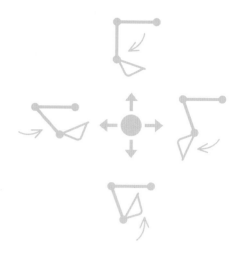

Some cranes have *telescopic* (*tel-eh-SKOP-ik*) arms. These arms can get longer or shorter. They can be used to reach places too high or dangerous for other cranes.

18

Telescopic arms look like they have many sections.

Cranes are busy at construction sites. They lower their cables to pick up giant metal beams. Then they lift the beams high in the air. Those beams are connected to other beams. Cranes keep lifting beams until the building is finished!

A magnet attached to a cable can lift heavy beams.

Activity: Be a Crane

Find a long piece of string or cord. Attach a tool to the end of it. Try a magnet, a hook, or something that can dig, like a toy shovel or spoon. Hold on to the string with your hand and use the tool to pick things up or dig a hole. Does it work better when your arm is bent or when your arm is stretched out?

Glossary

cab: the place where the operator sits

cable: a thick, heavy rope usually made of wire

Middle Ages: a time period in Europe from about 1,500 years ago to 500 years ago

operators: the people who control machines

salvage: to rescue a ship or other machine that has sunk underwater

telescopic: describing tubes or pipes that slide into one another

Read More About It

Llewellyn, Claire. *Mighty Machines: Truck.* New York: DK Publishing, 2000.

Martin, M. T. *Cranes.* Minneapolis: Bellwether Media, 2006.

Index